LONDON MIDLAND STEAM locomotives: 2

LONDON MIDLAND STEAM LOCOMOTIVES

A PICTORIAL SURVEY OF
EX-LMSR LOCOMOTIVES IN THE 1950s

VOLUME 2

BRIAN MORRISON

D. BRADFORD BARTON LIMITED

Frontispiece: Two veteran Johnson ex-Midland Railway 0-6-0s, dating from just before the turn of the century, photographed after coaling-up at Sheffield in August 1955. No.58225 is a Class 2F rebuilt in 1917 with Belpaire boiler and No.43388, classified 3F, was fitted with a Belpaire in 1916.

© copyright D. Bradford Barton Ltd 1975   ISBN 0 85153 200 4

printed in Great Britain by Chapel River Press (IPC Printers), Andover

for the publishers

D. BRADFORD BARTON LTD · Trethellan House · Truro · Cornwall · England

introduction

At the grouping of Britain's railways in 1923, the newly formed London Midland & Scottish Railway found itself with over 10,000 steam locomotives of very widely assorted designs, parentage and purpose. At Nationalisation in 1948 the company still had nearly 8,000 but by then there were only something like a 100 different classes left as against the myriad that had existed 25 years earlier. By the early 1950's on the Region, there was still something like 70 different classes remaining and these included not only engines built by the LMS itself but ex-Lancashire & Yorkshire, Caledonian, Highland and Furness types, as well as the obvious ones from the London & North Western and Midland Railways plus their earlier constituent lines such as the North London and London Tilbury & Southend.

Classifying locomotives as 3F, 4P or 5MT, etc. was an ideal arrangement from the operating standpoint but, to other than the specialist, it was often not apparent that Class 3F for example consisted of at least ten entirely different sub-classes which in turn also embraced several variations, of either major or minor importance. The general classification 2P involved some eight different types and even the ubiquitous Class 5MT included three different classes plus many varieties under the one umbrella. This volume, the second of two, illustrates at least one example of each class still working on the London Midland in the 1950's and in addition includes the majority of the varieties. Humbler and less well-known classes as well as those which were confined to working in more remote parts of the Region have deliberately been given greater prominence than the bigger and more popular wide-ranging or express types which are already adequately recorded elsewhere. On a similar basis, the short selection of locomotive workshop scenes at the conclusion of this Volume concentrates elsewhere than the well-known localities of Derby or Crewe. The illustrations are larger than has been seen before in a publication of this type and should appeal to railway modellers and LMS *aficionados*, plus those who just like to feast their eyes on the locomotive power variety that existed in the final decade of steam on British Railways. The photographs herein were taken in the 1950's before the change to dieselisation and were captured, in the main, whilst on shed. The locations are from as far north as Inverness and as far south as Templecombe—such was the size of the ex-LMSR system. This volume contains the locomotives numbered from 48000 onwards; the earlier ones, from 40000 to 47999 are in Volume 1.

Stanier's Class 8F 2-8-0s were introduced in 1935 and were to become the principal freight engine on the LMSR system. Weighing 72 tons 2cwt, the class had 18½in × 28in outside cylinders with Walschaerts valve gear, 4ft 8½in driving wheels and a taper boiler pressed to 225lb. The first 12 engines built in 1935 had domeless boilers and were, at first, classified as 7F. Rather grimy No. 48614 was photographed at its home shed, Nottingham (16A) in 1955.

Whilst a total of 666 engines came into BR stock in 1948 the Class 8Fs were, in fact, numerically the largest of all the Stanier locomotives, as 852 had been constructed in eleven years up to 1945. A larger number were built for use by the War Department during the second World War and many others were requisitioned from the LMS for use overseas and never returned. A few can still be seen to this day working in Iraq and Turkey. No. 48720, seen at Burton-on-Trent in 1955 shortly after being overhauled and repainted at Derby Works, was built at Brighton in the SR works there, in 1944, and worked on the LNER before passing to LMS ownership.

Bowen-Cooke's LNWR 'G1' Class 6F 0-8-0s were introduced in 1912 but many of them were rebuilds of earlier Whale and Webb 0-8-0s dating back to 1892. A second rebuilding came about from 1921 onwards when the original 160lb pressure boilers were replaced with 175lb Belpaire types, the classification being then increased to 7F, with these 0-8-0s becoming known as either 'G2' or 'G2a'. 'G2a' Class Nos. 49051 and 48943 are shown at Shrewsbury (84G) in July 1954 and August 1958 respectively. The last three of this once numerous class disappeared in 1964.

9

Originally consisting of 502 engines, the Class 6F and 7F 0-8-0s from the former LNWR still numbered 456 upon Nationalisation in 1948, although the earlier Class 'G1s' soon vanished, leaving some 275 of the class still active by the middle 1950's. (Above) No. 49129 seen at Wigan Springs Branch (10A) in 1955 was one of those fitted with a tender cab. Below, No. 49277 is by Willesden (1A) coaling stage in the same year.

Ex-LNWR 'G2' Class 7F 0-8-0 No. 49448 well coaled up outside Shrewsbury shed and soon to depart with a freight for South Wales. Although the 'G2s' were introduced in 1921 and the 'G2as' in 1936, both types presented the same general outward appearance and had the same basic dimensions—a weight of 62 tons, a boiler pressure of 175lb, 20½in × 24in cylinders, 4ft 5½in diameter driving wheels and a tractive effort of 28,045lb.

Sir Henry Fowler's Class 7F eight-coupled freight design was introduced on the L M S in 1929 and by 1932 a total of 175 of these locomotives were in service—far too many, most shed staff would say! Nicknamed 'Austin 7s', these were more or less a development of the older L N W R 0-8-0s but in service, principally due to bearing troubles, were not one of their designer's most successful engines. Scrapping commenced as early as 1949 and by the mid-1950's only 40 remained. No. 49664 is seen taking water at Liverpool Aintree (27B) shed.

No. 49648 (photographed at Wakefield (25A) in 1955), in line with the rest of the class, had a 200lb Belpaire boiler, 19½in × 26in cylinders, Walschaerts valve gear and 4ft 8½in wheels. By 1962 the class was extinct and it would be a fair epitaph on these 7Fs to say they were the unhappy outcome of a marriage between a first-rate boiler and a third-rate chassis. Freshly out-shopped, these were strong engines but mileage between repairs was lower than that of any other major LMS class.

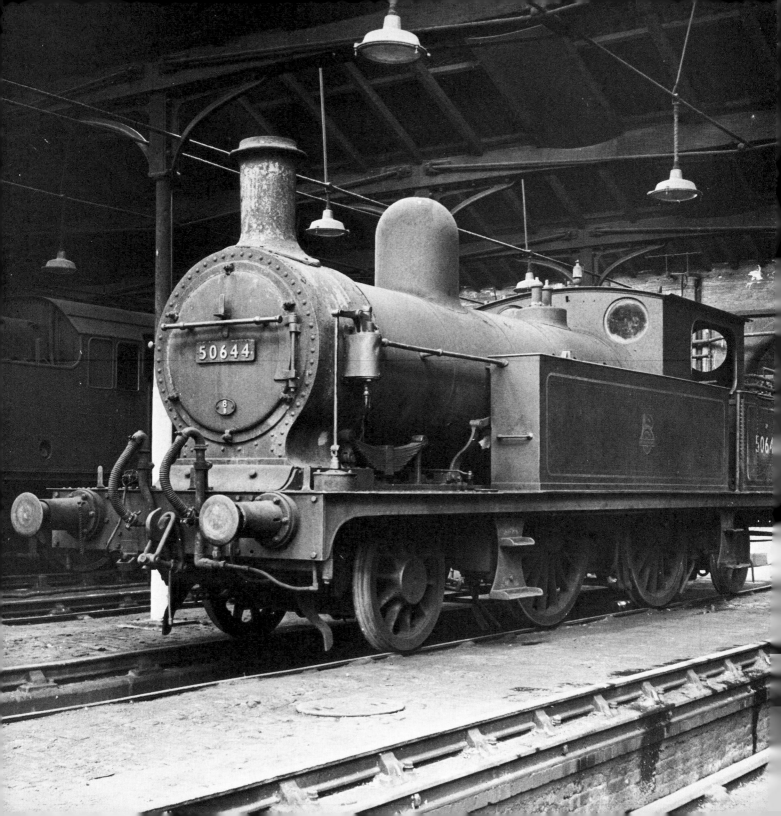

The Lancashire & Yorkshire Railway Class K2 2-4-2 tanks designed by Aspinall entered service in 1889 and were classified 2P under the LMS system. 309 had been built by 1910, the design being perpetuated by subsequent CMEs Hoy and Hughes. 110 of the class came into BR stock in 1948, of which 36 remained in service by 1955. No. 50652, seen in the gloom of Accrington shed (24A) in East Lancashire, was one of the class with 17in × 26in cylinders rebuilt with a Belpaire boiler in 1910, weighing 55 tons 19cwt and with a tractive effort of 18,360lb. No. 50644, with original type boiler, is inside Warrington shed (8B) and is of the type with larger (18in × 26in) cylinders and an increased tractive effort rated at 18,955lb.

15

Two further varieties of the Aspinall ex-L & Y 2-4-2Ts were those with the larger 18in × 26in cylinders which retained the original round-topped boiler, and the type introduced in 1898 with longer tanks, an extended smokebox and a 4 ton coal capacity (for the remainder of the class of two tons). All these types had a boiler pressure of 180lb and were fitted with Joy valve gear. No. 50660 of the first type described, is at Bolton (26C) in August 1955 and No. 50850, of the 1898 variety with weight increased to 59 tons 3cwt, is also at Bolton on the same day. These 2-4-2Ts were standard motive power on local-passenger turns everywhere in East Lancashire, virtually in every corner of the ex-L & Y system from Southport into Yorkshire.

Aspinall's little ex-L & Y 'B7' Class 0-4-0 saddle tanks were introduced in 1891 for working through the Liverpool dock area and the surrounding streets. 57 were constructed, of which 23 came into BR ownership in 1948. These 'Pugs', as they were called, were the smallest of all the L & Y engines and had a weight of 21 tons 5cwt, boiler pressure of 160lb, outside 13in × 13in cylinders, with 3ft $0\frac{3}{8}$in diameter wheels and a tractive effort of 11,335lb. After grouping in 1923, the class was distributed to a number of places far removed from their original Merseyside habitat. No.51237, with 'tin lid' spark arrester, is inside Bank Hall (27A) shed and No.51204, with drastically cut-down cab and chimney, in Widnes shed (8D). Despite the very rapid spread of diesel shunters, one of these 'Pugs' (No.51218, now preserved), survived into 1964.

The Aspinall ex-L & Y 'F16' Class 2F 0-6-0STs were 1891 rebuilds of Barton Wright's earlier Class F15, 0-6-0 tender engines built at Horwich in 1876. Of the original 280 locomotives, a total of 230 were turned into saddle tanks and 101 of these survived to Nationalisation in 1948. The last of these stalwarts was eventually withdrawn in 1964. No. 51447 was photographed at Manchester Newton Heath (26A) in the summer of 1956.

Bolton shed (26C), a real stronghold of the old L & Y, was home for No. 51484, a much cleaner Aspinall Class 2F, in 1955. The class had a weight in w.o. of 43 tons 17cwt, boiler pressure of 140lb, 17$\frac{1}{2}$in × 26in cylinders with Stephenson valve gear, 4ft 6in wheels and a tractive effort of 17,545lb.

The Lancashire & Yorkshire Class 'F20' 2F 0-6-0Ts designed by Aspinall were built in 1897 for use on dock lines. Of the original twenty engines, only five survived to Nationalisation. One of these, No. 51537, had the distinction of being the last engine in LMS stock to retain its pre-Nationalisation number—11537—which was not changed until September 1954. The only exceptions to this were five engines of the class described on the previous page that were used as shunters at Horwich Works, and were eventually scrapped without receiving the 40000 prefix. This photograph was taken in the cramped confines of the shed at Aintree (27B).

22

Tucked away at the back of Bank Hall shed (27A) with a 'Not to be moved' disc hanging out of the cab is another Aspinall 2F 0-6-0T. In common with the others in the class, No.51546 had outside 17in × 24in cylinders with Allan straight link gear, 140lb boiler pressure, 4ft wheels and a tractive effort of 15,285lb.

One of the very numerous Aspinall L & Y F 19 Class 0-6-0s, No. 52341, basks in the sunshine in September 1955 in the yards at Wigan Springs Branch. Other locomotives to be seen in the background are a Stanier 8F, a J 10 0-6-0 and a Stanier 2-6-4 tank.

24

Originally a class of 280 locomotives, 230 of these Barton Wright L&Y 'F15' Class 2F
0-6-0s were rebuilt as saddle tanks (see page 20) and of the remaining 50 engines,
25 came into BR ownership in 1948. By the mid-1950's only two remained, one of
them being grimy No. 52016 working out her last days shunting at Patricroft and
looking most of her 68 years of age. In line with the remainder of the class, No. 52016
weighed 39 tons 1cwt, had a boiler pressure of 140lb, 17½in × 26in cylinders and
Stephenson valve gear, and 4ft 6in diameter wheels.

The Lancashire & Yorkshire 'F19' Class 2F 0-6-0s by Aspinall were the most numerous of all types on this railway, with a total of 448 being constructed in the years between 1889 and 1917. 385 came into the LMS stockbook in 1923 and 234 of these useful all-rounder 2Fs remained at Nationalisation in 1948. The last example was scrapped during 1961. No.52186, in original condition with round-topped boiler and non-superheated, rests inside its home shed at Wakefield on 27 August 1955.

A view of ex-L & Y 0-6-0 No. 52278 at Liverpool Aintree (27B) in 1954, plainly showing the scanty Victorian cab which gave little protection against the elements. This class had a weight of 42 tons 3cwt, 18in × 26in inside cylinders, 180lb boiler pressure, 5ft 1in wheels and a t.e. of 21,129lb.

The basic Aspinall design was perpetuated by his successors, Hoy and Hughes, the later engines appearing with Belpaire fireboxes and an extended smokebox. No. 52413 of this type is seen at Lower Darwen (24D) shed in the summer of 1955.

Another of the Aspinall Class 2F 0-6-0s that was constructed under the Hughes era in 1911 with extended smokebox and Belpaire boiler, near Bolton in 1955; although in BR stock for seven years, No. 52132 still bears the legend 'LMS' on the tender. The specification of these locomotives was little different to the original types except that they had an increased weight (43 tons 11cwt).

Pettigrew Furness Railway Class 3F 0-6-0 No. 52510 stands out in the rain at Workington (12D) shed on 28 June 1957. Nineteen of this class were constructed between 1913 and 1920 of which six remained to carry a BR number. The later survivors were rebuilt with L&Y boilers, incorporating Belpaire fireboxes as illustrated, and these machines had a working weight of 44 tons 17cwt. The wheels were 4ft 7½in diameter, 170lb boiler pressure, and the two inside cylinders, fitted with Stephenson valve gear, measured 18in × 26in.

The Hughes L&Y 'F22' Class 3F 0-6-0s were rebuilds of the original 'F19s' described on pages 27 and 28 and were introduced in 1913. 63 of this simple but sturdy class were dealt with at Horwich Works in this way up to 1922 and 30 were left in 1948 to receive a BR number. 1957 saw the last withdrawal. The class was superheated and fitted with a Belpaire boiler of 180lb pressure, weighed 46½ tons and t.e. was quoted at 27,405lb. The wheels were 5ft 1in and the cylinders 20½in × 26in, with Joy valve gear. These two photographs of No.52575 were taken inside Bolton shed (26C) shortly before withdrawal.

The Somerset & Dorset Joint Railway's Class 7F 2-8-0s were designed for the company by Sir Henry Fowler in 1914 and the first six were delivered from Derby Works the following year. In 1925 a further five locomotives appeared, built by outside contractors, with 5ft 3in boilers compared to the 4ft 9in of the first six, but all were eventually rebuilt to the original specification. Engine weight was 64 tons 15 cwt, boiler pressure 190lb, outside cylinders 21in × 28in, driving wheels 4ft 8½in diameter, and t.e. 35,295lb. No. 53803 photographed on shed at Bath (71G) in April 1956 and the other two examples of the class (left), Nos. 53808 and 53804, at Templecombe (71H). This class gave excellent service on the S & D, being remembered with great affection by all who knew them. One has fortunately been preserved.

Peter Drummond's 'Small Ben' Class 2P 4-4-0s for the Highland Railway were built between 1898 and 1906. Half of the twenty built came into BR ownership at the date of Nationalisation but all were withdrawn by 1953. No. 54398 *Ben Alder* was scheduled for preservation but, after being stored for a number of years, it was unfortunately sent to the breakers in the late 1960's—whether by accident or design has never been really determined. The two photographs here were taken outside Inverness shed (60A) after *Ben Alder*'s withdrawal in July 1953. The class had an all-up weight of 46 tons 17 cwt, 6ft 0in driving wheels and $18\frac{1}{4}$in × 26in cylinders with Stephenson valve gear. Tractive effort was 17,890lb.

The McIntosh-designed Caledonian Railway 'Dunalastair' Class 3P 4-4-0s were probably the most famous of all the 1,000 or more locomotives inherited from that company by the LMS at the 1923 Grouping. 22 examples survived to enter BR stock and No.54439, photographed amid a Highland mist at its home shed of Wick (60D) in the summer of 1953, was the last to be withdrawn, in 1958. This locomotive, in fact, was one of two of the class that were superheated rebuilds of the original saturated 'Dunalastair IV' type and had a weight of 56 tons 10cwt, $20\frac{1}{4}$in × 26in cylinders and Stephenson valve gear, 6ft 6in driving wheels and 170lb boiler pressure. Constructed in 1907, they were rebuilt between 1915–17.

Known as the McIntosh 'Dunalastair IV Superheaters', the Caledonian '139' 4-4-0s were introduced in 1910 and 22 were constructed up to 1914. No. 54441 was of the first batch of six engines that had a 165lb boiler pressure, increased to 170lb in the later ones built, 20in × 26in cylinders as against 20¼ × 26in and a tractive effort of 18,700lb, slightly less than the 19,751lb of the later deliveries. All the class had a weight of 61 tons 5cwt and 6ft 6in diameter drivers. No. 54441 was in store at Greenock, Princes Pier (66D) when photographed in June 1957.

Having just emerged from Inverurie Works after a complete overhaul and repaint, Pickersgill Caledonian Class '72' 3P 4-4-0 No. 54507 poses for the camera on 25 June 1957.

All sixteen of Pickersgill's Caledonian Railway '113' and '928' Class 3P 4-4-0s, introduced in 1916, came into BR stock in 1948. Weighing 61 tons 5cwt, they had a boiler pressure of 175lb, 20in × 26in cylinders with Stephenson valve gear, 6ft 6in driving wheels and a tractive effort of 20,400lb. No. 54466 is seen inside Aviemore shed (60B) in July 1953 and No. 54468 at Greenock, Princes Pier (66D) in June 1957. The first withdrawals from the class took place in 1953 and the last survivor disappeared ten years later.

Last of the Pickersgill Caledonian '928' Class 3P 4-4-0s to be constructed, No. 54476, was stored at Perth (63A) when photographed in 1957. In all, Pickersgill introduced 48 various locomotives of this wheel arrangement between 1916 and 1922 and, although officially of three different classes, '72', '113' and '928' were all basically the same and appeared identical externally.

'72' Class 3P 4-4-0 No. 54503 at Perth. Whilst external differences between this class and the class '113' and '928' were almost impossible to discern, these engines had a higher boiler pressure (180lb), a slightly larger cylinder bore (20½in × 26in) and a greater tractive effort at 21,435lb. They were constructed 1920–22 and numbered 32 in the class. All came into BR ownership in 1948 and the last was withdrawn in 1963.

Drummond's Class 1P 0-4-4Ts on the Highland Railway were the last example of the line to remain in normal service. Four were built in 1905–6 and two of them survived to receive a BR number, their last days being spent working the Dornoch branch. No. 55053 was in course of overhaul in Lochgorm Works at Inverness in June 1957.

The McIntosh '92' Class 2P 0-4-4Ts were a class of 22 when introduced between 1897 and 1900 to the Caledonian Railway and, although 19 of them survived Nationalisation, they were soon withdrawn thereafter and only three remained by the mid-1950's. Originally built for the Glasgow Central low level lines, all were fitted with condensing gear as seen on No. 55126, acting as station pilot at Stirling in 1957. The others of the class had the condensers removed and, in addition, most received an ugly stovepipe chimney. They had a weight of 53 tons 19cwt, boiler pressure of 180lb, 18in × 26in cylinders and 5ft 9in driving wheels.

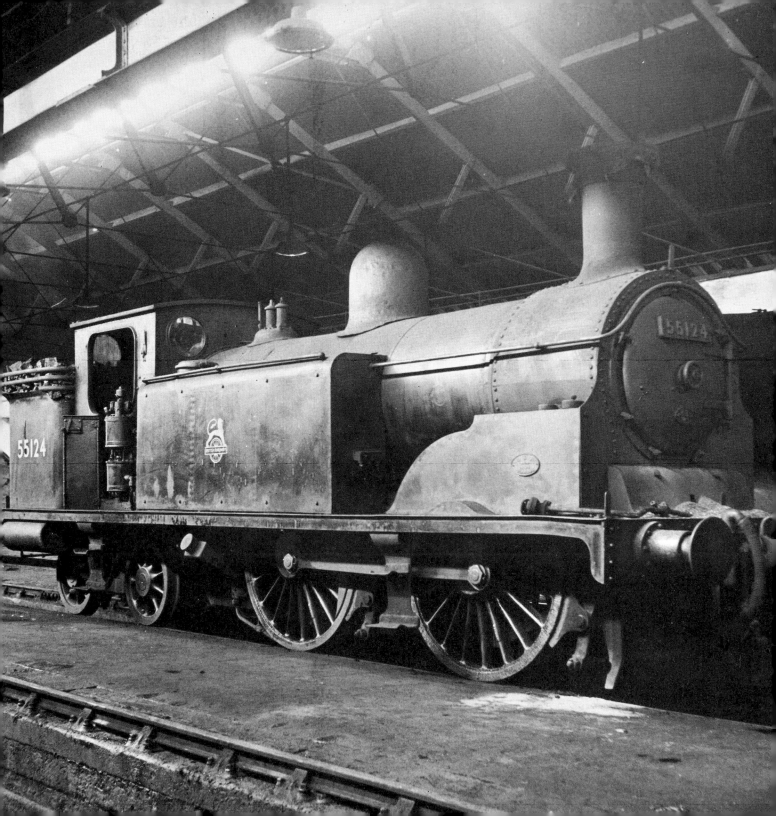

68 McIntosh Caledonian '439' Class 2P 0-4-4Ts were constructed between 1900 and 1914 and all but two came into BR stock in 1948. Their dimensions were the same as for the '92' Class detailed on an earlier page. No. 55217 is seen here at Thornton Junction (62A).

The McIntosh Caledonian '19' Class 2P 0-4-4Ts were constructed in 1895 and 7 of the 10 survived into the BR era. No. 55124 was the last survivor when photographed inside the shed at Dumfries (68B) in 1957, being finally withdrawn in 1961. The tanks were smaller than the high-sided ones fitted to the '92' Class but, apart from their weight of 53 tons 16cwt, other dimensions were the same.

Between 1915 and 1922 Pickersgill continued with production of the Class 439 'Standard Passenger' 0-4-4Ts introduced by McIntosh and a further ten were added to the original 68 of the Caledonian system, including No. 55227. Basic specifications were the same, with the exception of the weight which was increased to 57 tons 12cwt.

McIntosh '439' Class 2P 0-4-4T No. 55218 receiving major repairs in Lochgorm Works (Inverness) in July 1953, in company with Stanier 'Black Five' No. 45452.

The Caledonian '431' Class 2P 0-4-4Ts were specifically designed by Pickersgill for banking duties, four of them being produced in 1922. One of the class, No. 55237, photographed at Larkfield Sidings near Polmadie, was fitted with a stovepipe chimney. A minor point of interest is that these '431s' were fitted with special cast-iron front buffer beams.

No. 55239, sporting the much more attractive Caledonian chimney, also at Larkfield Sidings in June 1957. As with the others in the '431' Class, weight was 57 tons 17cwt and tractive effort 19,200lb. The remaining specifications were the same as the '439' class from which these engines were developed.

Last in the line of the numerous Caledonian Railway 0-4-4 tanks were the ten built in 1925 in LMS days after the Grouping, as a further development of the original McIntosh '439' Class first introduced at the turn of the century. The heaviest of the 0-4-4T series, these had a weight of 59 tons 12cwt, slightly larger cylinders (18½in × 26in) and a tractive effort the same as the Class 431 'Bankers', namely 19,200lb. The boiler pressure of 180lb and driving wheels 5ft 9in in diameter were in line with the earlier types. These two examples were photographed in June 1957, No. 55267 at Greenock Ladyburn (66D) and No. 55268 at Glasgow Polmadie (66A). No. 55267 has a slightly shorter type of stovepipe chimney.

McIntosh Caledonian Railway '498' Class 2F 0-6-0T No. 56173 at Greenock Ladyburn in 1967. This class, consisting of 23 locomotives, was designed principally for dock shunting and is described on page 62.

Dugald Drummond's Caledonian Railway Class OF 0-4-OSTs came onto the scene in 1878 and successive batches were constructed up to 1908 to bring the class total to 39. Fourteen survived to Nationalisation, the last one not being withdrawn until as late as 1962—a life-span for the class of a remarkable 84 years. The big roundhouse at Inverness was home for No. 56038—with early style of BR lettering—and No. 56011, in July 1953. Being Sunday, they are resting from their normal local shunting duties. The combination of sprung buffers added to the original dumb-buffers gave these short wheelbase tanks a considerable overhang and they were extremely lively across pointwork.

Used at St. Rollox as the Works shunter, No. 56025 was maintained in beautiful condition, as can be seen in this photograph dating from June 1957. The Class OF 'Pugs' weighed 27 tons 7cwt, had a boiler pressure of 160lb, 3ft 8in wheels, 14in × 20in cylinders, with a tractive effort of 12,115lb.

Even the fitting of a stovepipe chimney did little to mar the attractiveness of these diminutive machines; No. 56031 is seen here at Greenock Ladyburn in 1957. Note the large diameter buffers as compared with the St. Rollox Works shunter opposite.

The McIntosh '498' Class 2F 0-6-0Ts were built at St. Rollox between 1911 and 1921 and all 23 of these Caledonian locomotives came into BR ownership in 1948. Designed with a short wheelbase for use as dock shunters, the engines had a working weight of almost 48 tons, 4ft diameter wheels and a tractive effort of 18,015lb. No. 56157, with stovepipe chimney, and No. 56163, with the original Caledonian type, were photographed at Greenock Ladyburn in 1957. The last of the class to be condemned was No. 56159 in 1962.

The McIntosh
Class '29' 3F 0-6-0Ts
were not very large
locomotives but
compared to their
fellow Caledonian
Railway 'Pugs' they
appeared quite
sizable; No. 56291,
one of the few of
the class retaining
a Caledonian chimney,
on shed at Inverness
in 1953 alongside
No. 56038.

Caledonian '782' Class 3F 0-6-0 No. 56262 in service as one of the yard shunters at Inverness, June 1957. Built between 1895 and 1922, these engines and the '29' Class were grouped together and the specifications detailed overleaf were the same. 147 were built in all and the whole of this useful and hardworking class came into BR stock at Nationalisation. The last withdrawals took place in 1962 following the spread of dieselisation on Scottish Region.

The McIntosh '29' and '782' Class 3F 0-6-0Ts weighed 47 tons 15cwt, had 4ft 6in wheels, a boiler pressure of 160lb, 18in × 26in cylinders with Stephenson valve gear and t.e. of 21,215lb; No. 56336 at Grangemouth (65F) in 1957 and No. 56308 at Polmadie in 1956.

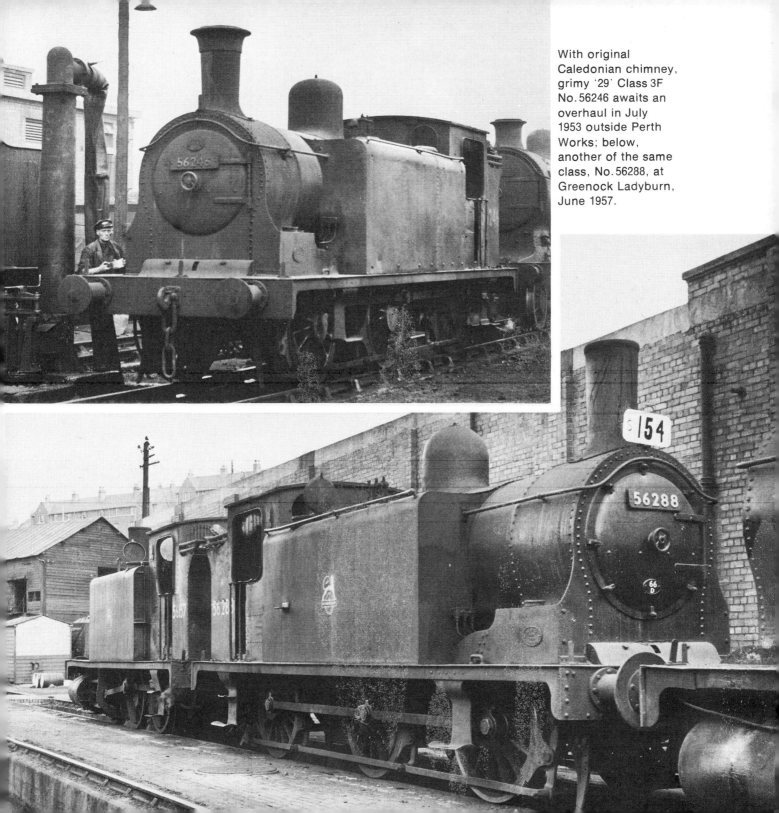

With original Caledonian chimney, grimy '29' Class 3F No. 56246 awaits an overhaul in July 1953 outside Perth Works; below, another of the same class, No. 56288, at Greenock Ladyburn, June 1957.

Dugald Drummond's 'Jumbo' Class 0-6-0s were numerically the largest on the Caledonian with 244 being constructed between 1883–97 and the class being perpetuated by CMEs Smellie, Lambie and McIntosh. All came into LMS ownership in 1923 and no less than 238 survived into BR days. Some of the class were rebuilt with an LMS boiler, one of them being No. 57239, photographed at Polmadie in 1957. Fresh out from the paint shop at Inverurie Works, No. 57273 (opposite) awaits return to its home depot at Dawsholm (65D) in the same year. This engine retains the much more handsome Caledonian chimney.

A few 'Jumbos' were specially fitted with condensing apparatus for the Glasgow Central low level lines, as shown on No. 57473 seen at Perth (63A) in 1957. It will be observed how much more elegant these popular locomotives looked when they retained the designer's original type of chimney.

'Jumbo' Class 2F 0-6-0 No.57384, of Hamilton (66C) shed, rests at Perth on a mid-summer day in 1957. The chimney and dome are slightly cut down as compared with the example of the same class on page 68 but the basic specifications remain identical, the inside cylinders being 18in × 26in, with Stephenson valve gear, wheels 5ft 0in diameter, boiler pressure 180lb and tractive effort 21,480lb.

Caledonian '812' Class 3F 0-6-0 No.57552 was one of a class of 96 locomotives constructed between 1899 and 1909, incorporating the '652' Class 3F 0-6-0s illustrated overleaf, whose specifications were exactly the same. All of the class came into LMS stock and 93 survived into BR ownership. They had a weight of 45 tons 14cwt, 5ft 0in wheels, inside $18\frac{1}{2}$in × 26in cylinders, 180lb boiler pressure and a tractive effort of 22,690lb.

McIntosh '812' Class 3F 0-6-0 No. 57597 at Keith (61C) shed in July 1953. Alongside is Pickersgill Great North of Scotland Railway D40 Class 4-4-0 No. 62264.

An example of the McIntosh Caledonian '652' Class 3F 0-6-0s that had the same specification as the '812' Class (described on page 72)—No.57631, seen at Glasgow St. Rollox in June 1957.

Pickersgill's Caledonian '294' Class 3F 0-6-0s were built from 1918-20 and 43 examples were produced. All came into LMS ownership in 1923 and 29 into BR ownership. The last was withdrawn in 1963. No.57653 (with a smaller than normal steam dome) was photographed at Carlisle Kingmoor (68A) and No.57682 at Greenock Princes Pier.

The second batch of MR 0-4-4Ts was introduced in 1881, with slightly smaller (5ft 4in) driving wheels and a tractive effort of 14,460lb as compared with the 13,810lb of the earlier 1875 series. In all, Johnson was responsible for 205 tanks of this type, of which 65 survived to Nationalisation. No. 58054, one of the type with a boiler pressure of 140lb, is seen here at Emerson Park Halt on the Romford–Upminster service in July 1952.

No. 58038, the last survivor of the first series of Midland Class 1P 0-4-4Ts with 5ft 7in driving wheels, photographed near Romford on a train to Upminster, September 1953. The class, designed by Johnson, dated from 1875.

76

The final series of Johnson Class 1P 0-4-4Ts were constructed just before the turn of the century. With increased (150lb) boiler pressure, they produced a tractive effort of 15,490lb. All these 0-4-4Ts weighed 53 tons 4cwt and were fitted with 18in × 24in inside cylinders actuated by Stephenson valve gear. No. 58065 was working out its last days on the Southwell–Rolleston Junction branch line when photographed at Lincoln shed (40A) on 24 May 1959.

Fowler's massive ten-coupled 'Lickey Banker' was introduced in 1919 for work on the formidable 1 in 37 Lickey incline in the Midlands. Weighing 73 tons 13cwt, this sole example of its type had a boiler pressure of 180lb, four 16¾in × 28in cylinders with Walschaerts valve gear, 4ft 7½in diameter wheels and a tractive effort of 43,315lb. Apart from the Garratts, this was the most powerful of L M S R locomotives and in appearance considerably resembled the Fowler 7F 0-8-0s but it gave far better service than the latter—perhaps due to a lesser annual mileage on restricted Lickey use. The tender cab, similar to those originally provided with the S & DJ 2-8-0s, continued to be used throughout the life of No. 58100, being useful for the crews' comfort when running back down the gradient tender first.

Johnson ex MR Class 2F 0-6-0 No. 58246 inside Burton-on-Trent (17B) shed on 28 August 1955. At this date, this was the last to survive of the original type introduced in 1875 with a round-top boiler, the remainder having been rebuilt with Belpaire boilers. The enormous total of 935 of the class was constructed up to 1908 for the Midland and all these came under the LMS in 1923. Rapid inroads into them were made, however, with the end of the 'small engine' policy, yet by Nationalisation 603 still remained. By the 1950's the class had been reduced to just over 100. Weighing 40 tons and with 4ft 11in wheels, these locomotives had 160lb boiler pressure, inside 18in × 26in cylinders and produced a nominal t.e. of 19,420lb.

From 1917 onwards Johnson's Midland Class 2F 0-6-0s were rebuilt with Belpaire boilers and two such examples are seen here. No.58162, at Shrewsbury in July 1954, was of the series with 4ft 11in wheels, weighing 40 tons and having a t.e. of 19,420lb, whereas No.58207 had 5ft 3in diameter wheels and t.e. of 18,185lb. The legend 'LMS' is still visible on the tender. Both engines have been fitted with the later Deeley cab.

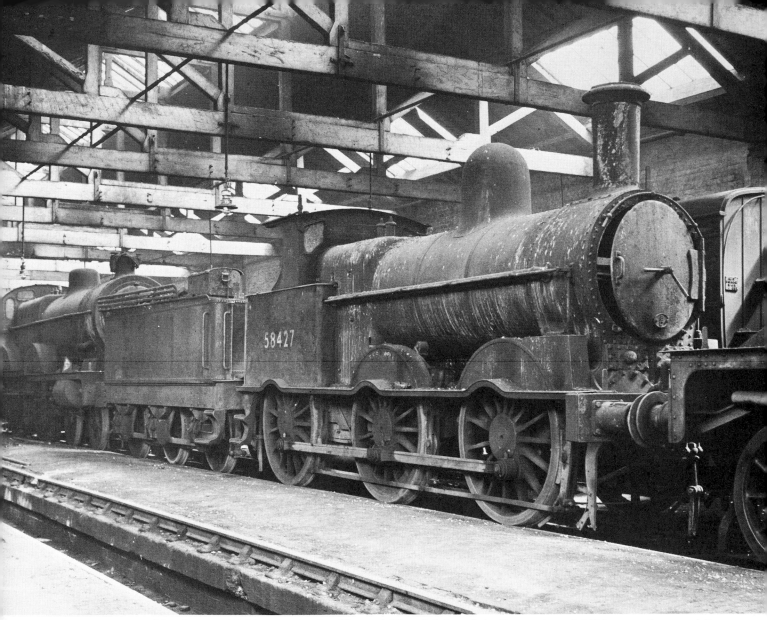

The famous Webb L N W R 'Cauliflower' Class 0-6-0s originally numbered 310 locomotives and these were built between 1880-1902. All but two came into LMS stock in 1923 but only 69 remained at Nationalisation in 1948. The final one to be condemned, in December of that year, was No. 58427, seen in store inside Trafford Park (9E) shed on 24 August 1955. The 'Cauliflowers' weighed 36 tons 10cwt and produced a t.e. of 15,865lb. Boiler pressure was 150lb and wheel diameter 5ft 2in. With the official L N W R title of '18in Goods', the cylinders were naturally of that diameter but, in fact, most had been lined down to 17½in or 17in for many years. All were fitted with Joy valve gear, which was largely responsible for their characteristic exhaust note, aptly described as sounding rather like a 'steamy contralto.''

The thirty North London Railway Class 2F 0-6-0Ts were built between 1887–1905 and all these entered service with the LMS at the Grouping. Fourteen survived to 1948 and the last, No. 58850, was withdrawn in 1960 but has been preserved and now runs on the Bluebell Railway. Weight was 45 tons 10cwt, boiler pressure 160lb, outside cylinders 17in × 24in with Stephenson valve gear; the wheels were 4ft 4in diameter and t.e. 18,140lb. No. 58854 was recorded at Devons Road (1D) on 16 April 1955.

Stripped of the side tanks, North London Class 2F 0-6-0 No. 58859 is hardly recognisable undergoing a major overhaul at Bow Works, 16 April 1955.

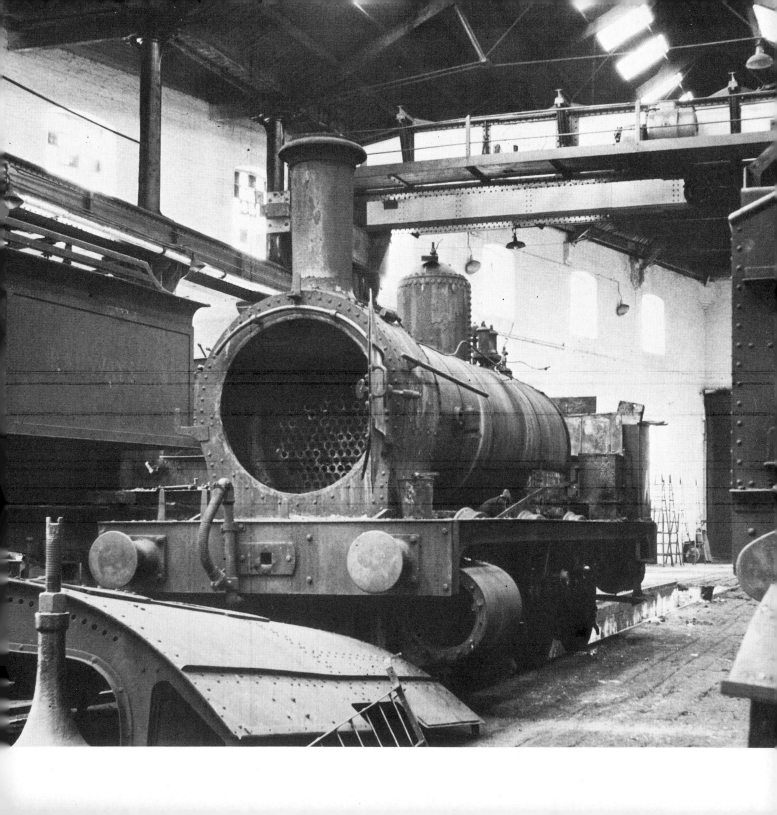

The North London Class 2F 0-6-0Ts in their last years were all allocated either to Devons Road (1D) or to Rowsley (17D) and one or more could always be seen at either location up to their final withdrawal. No.58857 was photographed at the London shed in October 1955.

Webb's 'Coal Tank' Class 2F 0-6-2Ts were built by the LNWR between 1881 and 1896 and at their peak the class numbered 300. All but 9 survived to LMS days and 64 came into BR stock in 1948. The last was withdrawn in 1958 but is happily now preserved as No.1054 in LNWR lined black livery. Seen in store at Abercynon in South Wales on 26 May 1955 are No.58891 and the now preserved No.58926. These 'Coal Tanks' weighed 43 tons 15cwt, had 4ft 5½in driving wheels, 150lb boiler pressure, 17in × 24in cylinders and a t.e. of 16,530lb.

Receiving attention inside Perth Works in July 1953, Pickersgill Class 3P 4-4-0 No. 54502 and North British Class D30/1 4-4-0 No. 62426 *Cuddie Headrigg.*

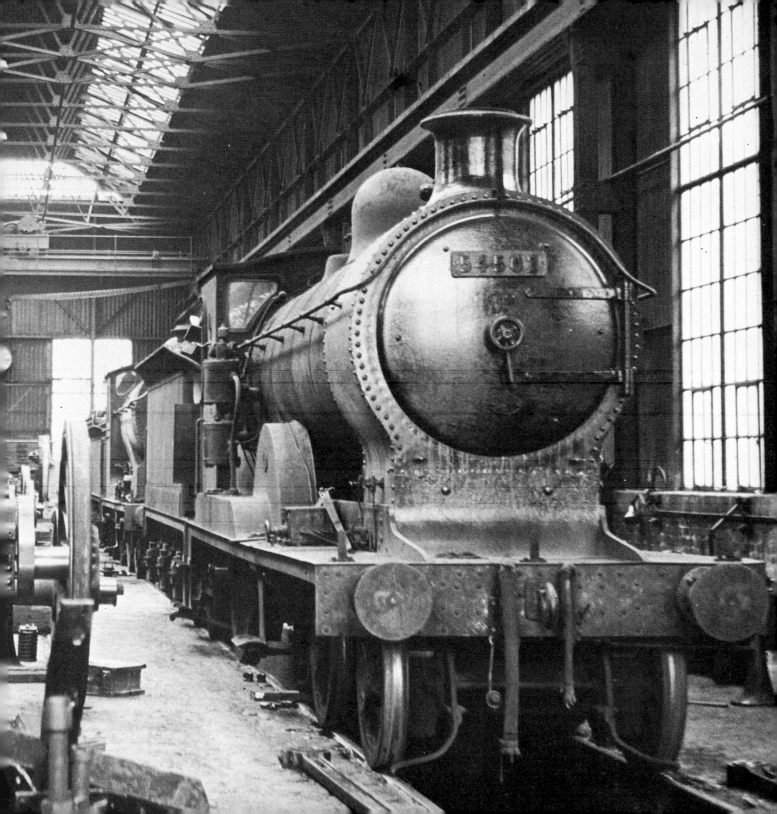

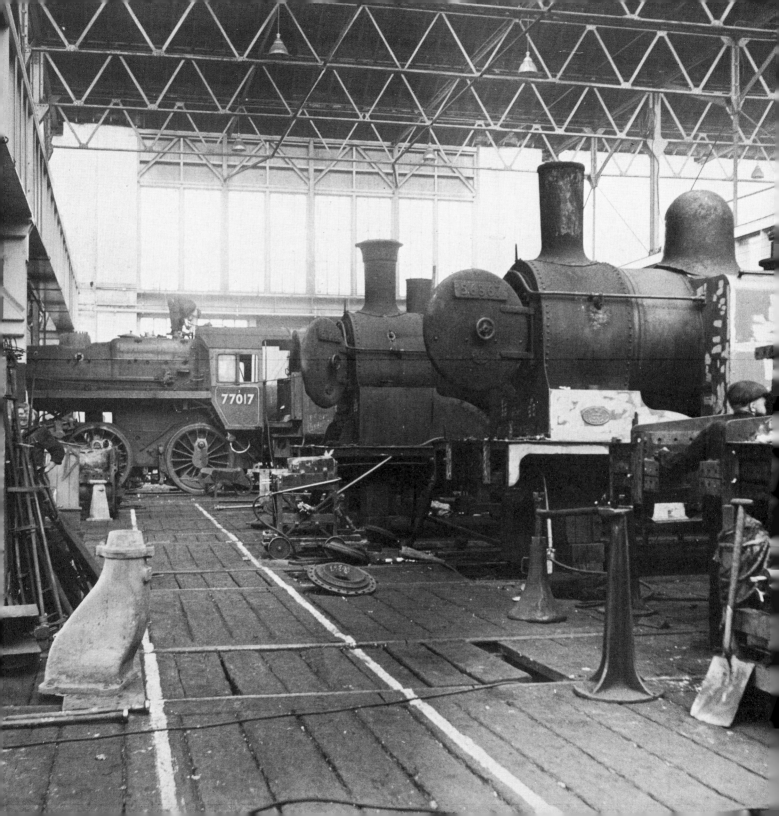

McIntosh Caledonian Railway '812' Class 3F 0-6-0 No. 57601 undergoing overhaul at St. Rollox Works, Glasgow in 1957. Opposite: old and new at Inverurie Works in the same year; B R Standard Class 3MT 2-6-0 No. 77017 contrasts with Caledonian '431' Class 0-4-4-T No. 55238 and '29' Class No. 56367, all undergoing heavy repair.

Ex-Midland Railway Class 3F 0-6-0 No. 43729 and Stanier 3-cylinder 2-6-4T No. 42514 under overhaul in April 1955 in Bow Works, London.

An Ivatt Class 4MT 2-6-0 receives attention outside Stratford Works, London, in August 1954. All the valve gear and connecting rods have been removed and the boiler tubes are also partly withdrawn.

Another scene inside the North London Works at Bow in 1955 with five locomotives under repair. From left to right can be seen Class 3F 0-6-0T No. 47487, ex-LT & SR 3P 4-4-2T No. 41941, a Johnson Midland 3F 0-6-0, another 'Jinty' and another LT & SR Atlantic tank.

ome LMS designs travelled to other regions and here Fairburn Class 4MT 2-6-4T No. 42082, allocated ɔ the Southern Region, receives attention at Bricklayers Arms Works in April 1955.

Overleaf: LMS steam lives on! Restored to LMS livery, Stanier Class 8F 2-8-0 No. 8233 glints in the autumn sunshine at Bridgnorth on the Severn Valley Railway in 1973.